Illustrations by

Martha Mendoza

Photography by

John J Roche

Copyright © 2008 by John J Roche

ISBN 978-1-4357-1997-2

John J Roche

A special thanks to Marilyn Ogella and Janice de Hart

For all their support encouragement and advice

4

Jim and Agnes

PTMN

John J Roche

The Flax in Bloom

The Flax in Bloom is a well known reel amongst Irish traditional players. Traditional musicians love to play reels and jigs. Irish music is composed on the instrument, that is, for centuries they have composed tunes and handed down by ear to the next generation without ever being committed to paper. In this way the music remains alive; each generation adding their own variations. It is a relatively new practice, in terms of the long history of the music, that written collections have been made. Traditionally Irish musicians have always given their compositions names. The name given to a tune normally reflects something concerning the life of the composer.

Flax was a very important commodity in Ireland due to the lively linen trade. The composer of the tune more than likely either grew the flax or worked with it in some form.

Flax has been a very important commodity in the history of civilization. It was known in the Ancient Near East as far back as 5000 BC from the Mediterranean to India and extensively grown on the Banks of the Nile and as the Hymn to Hapi has it: *People are clothed with the flax of his fields* (M.Lichtheim *Ancient Egyptian Literature*, Vol.1, p.207). Flax requires a moderate moist climate as provided by the Nile delta. Flax was the fibre of choice because wool was too hot for Egypt and cotton was unknown there.

A portion of the crop was harvested just before the grain harvest when the flax was in full bloom as this practice produced better fibre. It was longer and stronger than any other they could grow and was spun into yarn for making clothes. The Flax that had been left in the field was a source of seeds for next year and the courser fibres from these shoots went into the creation of bags, twine and rope.

Down through the years various parts of the plant have been used to make linseed oil, fabric, dye, paper, medicines, fishing nets and soap. Today flax seeds are in demands for their essential heart healthy Omega 3 rich oil.

John J Roche

Poems

8

John J Roche

John J Roche

A Simple Thought

When your clay leadens

And you drag wearily

Under the dark

May a simple thought or smile

Awaken; kindle and enliven

When your spirit's lassitude

Dampens any hint of colour

To a panoramic grey sepia

May a simple thought or smile

Bring a flock of colours Red, Green and Indigo Blue

When living or non-living

Fascinates no compulsion

Living dead maybe

May a simple thought or smile

Be a morsel for life; a midwife's slap

When days are eternal

A torture of long minutes

Counts out bland days

May a simple thought or smile

Billow your sail with a fresh urgent breeze

John J Roche

Solutions seem impossible to snare

Lost in countless matrices of sleepless turning

May a simple thought or smile

Be a strong starting corner piece

In the puzzle of life

When that crack of light blue

Crazes the world of gray

A proleptic glimpse of promise

May it have been a simple thought or smile

That warmed your soul with a scattered rainbow

Hospitality

The truly open door sports no latch

The generous welcomes with delight

Only he who has made space in his heart

Has room to welcome in the guest

He who is full of opinions and moralisations

Has no room to take anyone under his roof

He who has welcomed his own brokenness

Can bear his brother's shadow

He who has naught but a warm heart

Will invite others to warm themselves at his hearth

Unconditional acceptance of the other

Gives true hospitality and freedom to be

John J Roche

Alexander The Great

The Macedonian's most praised son

Eleven cities baptised in his name; by the sword.

Jealously anguished over Philip's conquests

Would there be anything left to be won?

Ruling Greek kingdoms like Poseidon and Agenor

He extended dominion over the men of the East

With battlefield innovation

The iron and bronze fist held all Asia Minor

Exploits of such warriors takes one's breath

And speaks directly to the hearts of young men

Who would themselves conquerors be

But, there is a price: an early death

John J Roche

T E Lawrence

A Dangerous man who dreamed with his eyes open

Assertive voices, from podiums, declare

That all who lay their head to sleep

Journey far and wide in their deep

Until the morn to consciousness repair

Like Jacob with his nocturnal wrestler spent

A night in combative torment

Or, accumulating ideas to ferment

Once the veil of night is rent

Resolutions taken from night's seering

Lack compulsion and straight forward steering

Lawrence dared dream in daylight's vision

A new order in detailed precision

He who with Herculean spirit strives and dares

Will sculpt the dream that all will see clear

Betrayal

As deadly as callously dispensed hemlock

Leprous sensibility accompanies administration;

Ice blood flowing through eyes that do not balk

Such is the one who kisses and stabs simultaneously

Who hammered three nails into my feelings

Whose honeyed words were pleasant but truthless.

So take care to whom you entrust your heart

Let reason puncture love's blindness

Imitate not Don Juan but Rene Descartes

John J Roche

Carpe Diem

As I roved out one morning fair

Along the banks of the Nore

A handsome lass was taking the air

With a garland in her hand

Being bold I said I'll walk with you a while

And be a guide for you this day

Confessed; the fairest I'd seen in this Isle

And proud I'd be to walk with her for ever and a day

A brighter star for me than the sun

Lit and lightened every step

Stunned; like one hit on the head

My heart cried valiantly "hook this one"

Niddering would not win a hand this day

Oh to be bold and brave like the poet warriors

Rout the defense and capture the prey

With a stolen kiss in a meadow of hay

John J Roche

The Blood On The Rose

Solitary she stands

Contrasting rustic hues

The White Rose

Attracts the eye

Her dazzling beauty

Is well barbed

Brave and fool

Chance the thorn

Stabbing and piercing

She draws blood

Any great prize

Taken too easily

Is soon discarded

John J Roche

Rainbow

Ruby lips

Orange sunsets

Yellow lamplight

Green eyes

Blue jeans

Indigo moods

Violet water

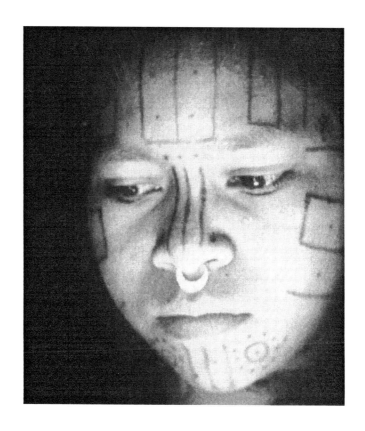

John J Roche

Two Coins for the Ferryman

What did you think of as you closed your eyes for the last time?

What vision did you have to take with you?

Did it comfort and sustain you?

What was it like to feel your body growing cold?

What was it like to feel the rigours?

Were you lonely as you lay cold on the marble?

What was it like lying in the coffin?

Was there fear in eyes that we did not see?

Was it frightening to hear the lid being screwed down?

Could you hear the priest's words of comfort over you?

Did you hear the Aves?

Could you smell the incense and hear the tears?

John J Roche

What did you think of the kind things said of you?

What did you think of the people who said them?

Did you hear my tears of love?

What was it like to be laid deep in the clay?

Did it feel cold and damp?

Did you panic at being entombed in the earth?

Will you miss me as I miss you?

Will you keep me in your love as I do you?

Will you think often of me as I do you?

I miss you old friend and wonder how you are.

John J Roche

The Song Of The Soul

Deep within the soul whispers delicately

Only to be drowned under the pitch of everyday

With discordant syncopations blaring hollow promises

Distract and veil the cadence of the soul

The song of the soul stirs in the bones

No shallow lyrics over a catchy bass beat

It is composed in soft hushed timbre

Echoing the small soft still still enunciations

To leave the tinsel world and journey deep

To adopt the grammar of silence and stillness

To enter within core's central keep

To find the real self in tranquility and quietness

John J Roche

Lunch Date

Glass panel doors invite into an ambiance of elegance

Greeted by a perfunctory welcome of well
rehearsed lines

Led through a maze of random diners;

Women nattering, business men bantering noisily
over salads and lovers huddled in séance;

A mother and daughter sifting their bargain
hunting

Settled. Eyes engage flickering and coy; speaking
silent thoughts

Communicating in the grammar of signal;
complicated semaphore of deeper appetites

Consumed in their conversation. A phone nearby
rings in distracting manner; causing a frown

An annoying waiter hovers and interrupts; choose
from an array of Italy's regional delights.

Celebrating her anniversary of the midwife's slap

Gifts are conjured; pale tokens of the heart

At a tear of joy my heart did quake

Clocks stopped as we consumed our stolen moments

Time has flown as we step back from this our moment of eternity

T'was not the wine that had intoxicated me

Nor anything ingested that warmed my heart

But only my fondness for you

And it was your embrace that did make my heart race

A perfect day only because I was with you

Experience

Many a truth I wish to tell

That life has schooled me well

Pain writes the memory a note

Deeper and quicker than by rote

Pearls I cast but few will take

Especially the young or the rake

The pain of one generation

Brings to the next no redemption

They cry "why did you not tell me"

You knew too much to listen to oldies like me

John J Roche

Ashling

Red fingers stretch and elongate, jabbing at the heart
of the dark
Cocks crow, quadrupeds stretch and straighten,
wringing out the night's slumber
The still silence of the dark overtaken by the noise of
waking and the lark
Spines creak out the last of night's stiffness and the
nocturnals clamber for their chamber

The red dawn lingers short; morphing orange to
yellow
Consciousness stirs my twilight mind and it ponders -
What day? T'is today!
Soon white light floods and invades every corner and
gone are the shadows soft and mellow
My heart is joyful for today my star will shine brighter
than the sun to light my heart

My star illuminates my soul and spirit with the warmth
of soft loving light
Through a prism her light demonstrates degrees of
gentle radiant beauty and charms
Like gold at rainbow's end so illusively sought; is my
plight
The treasure I hunger for and long to cup and trap
forever in my arms

But *todays* are short and my star retreats leaving a deep
longing
The solitude and loneliness of the night returns in the
absence of my star for light
Longing for that eternal day when snuggled in my arms
forever remaining
To banishing forever night and darkness with her
intoxicating light

The Dinner Party

Warm glows flicker from the well banked fire

Dance their welcomes on the walls

Aromatic announcements of the cuisine

Titivate and foster delightful expectations

Warm glows from mulled red wine

Expels the winter damp

Soft spoken tones crescendo with legion

Idle frivolous chatter consuming attention

Warm glows from intimate table covenant

Tugs tighter the strings of friendship

Toasting their alliances with every glass

Intoxicating friendliness with time well passed

Warm glows from hearts and souls enjoined

Lasting satiety spans the gaps of time

Central is this to life and living

Life's nexus is ne'er toil but relation

John J Roche

Warm glows from memories deep within

Bridge the barren days of absence

Let us always eager be for new memories

Ever creating and deepening friendships

John J Roche

Eve's Apple

Was it just plain curiosity, or,

Was it defiance of prohibition

That drove her to bite?

Is it a trait of nature

That riles against rules, or,

Is it just plain curiosity that drives us mad?

No matter the reason, bite she did

Curiosity the woman's downfall

Seduction the man's

The culprits called to a reckoning

"Not I" the defense

Laying blame at the other's door

John J Roche

Abdication of responsibility

Has since been the order of the day

And will be from the first Adam to the last

Eros Danced

Eros danced whene'er we met

Snaring our hearts with threads of love

> A bronze thread of affection

> A silver thread of friendship

> A golden thread of faithfulness

Dancing and twirling he platted the threads

'Til our hearts locked fast; now perpetual togetherness

John J Roche

Far Away

When I'm far away from thee

My lovely

I miss your smile and laugh

My lovely

I miss the touch of your petite hand

My lovely

Those soft small hands that fit snugly in mine

My lovely

My arm misses holding you tight to me

My lovely

My eye misses staring into your warm soul

My lovely

I miss the laughter in your eye

My lovely

I miss your playfulness

My lovely

But most of all I miss your lips on mine

John J Roche

Bonnie Kate

Oh beautiful and lovely your eyes

Oh beautiful and lovely your smile

Oh beautiful and lovely your nature

Oh beautiful and lovely your gentle way

Oh beautiful and lovely your soft caress

Oh beautiful and lovely your tender embrace

John J Roche

A Day For Rising

The call was given and answered stoutly

Davids gathering before the invading Goliaths

Brave and bold they stood defiant to man

That Easter in the GPO*

Slow bloodletting of freemen

Weakened by many a blow

Frail but proud they marched out

Heads high, hands high, for liberty

General Post Office, Dublin, 1916

50

This feast of rising is remembered well

Freedom's nail was hammered true

Inspiring a nation with

Infectious dreams of liberty

Blood and dreams was our mother

Born through struggle and travail

Heroes glad to bear this pain

For cherished freedom and liberty

Afternoon

A soft gentle current transports the scent of late summer

Violets, horse chestnuts, lilac and flowers of every hue

The heathery breeze, soft and warm, gently caresses

A meadow of colours green, red, brown, yellow and
indigo blue

Midges come out to dance with darting flair

Shadows lengthen on the meadow as a blush of rouge
tinges the sky

Smoke curling and wafting gracefully in the evening air

A red western glow signals the ebb of day

John J Roche

Adam's Seed

I am Paris who fought and fell at Troy for Helen

I am Diarmuid who made the Dolman's to shelter Grainne

I am Samson who was beguiled by Delilah

I am Abelard who was smitten by Eloise

I am Shakespeare's Romeo who rather'd death to separation

I am Heathcliffe who was one with the Cornish lass Cathy

I am the Oxford don, Lewis, who was turned head over heel by his American friend

I am John Denver whose senses tingled like a night in the forest by thoughts of Annie

Yes, I am everyman who has ever lived and loved

Driven by the same deep powers to hold and caress

Whose reason has been confounded by love's logic

When blood is boiled by love

We are fired into life by love
And exist only by it

John J Roche

Lough Derg

Patrick made his own Purgatory

For days of purgation and mortification

On the Lough of Derg

A barren bleak crag

Fraught with denial and abstinence

To harden the soul

The prayer of this Purgatory

One hundred and fifty Aves

One hundred and fifty times

No comfort on this granite crucible

Barefoot on bare rocks reminds

'Tis the narrow way that is hard

Mortified reflections weigh

That between two worlds we hang

Everyman

I am the negro, the oriental, the caucasian

The businessman, the artist, the secretary

The floor sweeper, the teacher, the tradesman

From pole to pole or from here to Timbuktu

Culture and history qualifies a cosmic vista

But, essentially what I am you are too

Only in the mind am I different to everyman

Imaginary lines drawn on a globe to divide

On the surface only melanin dictates a clan

John J Roche

Sliabh Bloom

One fine June day roaming in the vale of the Sliabh
Bloom

Tracing the meandering and winding conduit of the
Nore

Gallivanting o'er grazing pastures of a thousand subtle
hues

Ditched and hedged with ash, elm, oak or bonnie yews

Humming a melody penned by the mighty Moore*

Reminded me of my honey sweet; a lovely for sure

There's no beauty as her in hill, vale, plain or moor

*Thomas Moore, 1779-1852, published a 10 volume work Irish
Melodies. It was translated into every European language including
Polish and Russian

Every young man has an eye for the native shrew

Even if dimmed by indulgence of distilled or brew

All would consent that she is finer than pure gold ore

Ne'er have I felt such desire from the day I left the womb

As that day I spied this fair maid on the banks of the Nore

No better rib would e'er I find if I traveled a thousand miles or more

From Dundalk to Dingle or even Malin to Macroom

John J Roche

The Hills of Distant Longing

At yonder meadow's skirt

Rise the hills of distant longing

Under a summer's western sunglow

A vista more glorious and appealing

Than this field wherein I plod and sweat my brow

Those hills of distant longing

Entice perennial bidding

Wistful dreams in the dead of night

Tantilise and conjure a conquering hero

To a life both new and bright

They invite like forbidden fruit

Churning up the inward fray

In madness and sorrow I clenched my fist

In frustration I drown by resisting those distant lures

For responsibility and timidity is my grist

All my youth I sought those far lying hills

And in the slowing days of my autumn

I discovered, after visiting the dark wood

That the promises of those distant hills

Were always under my roof; years lost longing.

John J Roche

Samsara

In my infancy I was helpless, vulnerable and dependant

In my childhood I soaked up the wonders of the world

In my adolescence I became awkward in company

In my late teens I saw myself becoming the hero

In my twenties I discovered commitment

In my thirties I treasured my possessions

In my midlife I entered Dante's tangled wood

In my life now I see what should have mattered all along

It's the who not the what that is truly pivotal

Now as I move towards my senior years

I will become helpless, vulnerable and dependant

John J Roche

The Music Man

Isolated by the single shaft of light

Accompanied only by his old Gibson

His hands move over it as comfortably as a lover

Together they resonate harmoniously

Alone in his nervousness

Alone in his critical thoughts

Alone in his anxiety to please

Alone is his craving for adulation

The ice is broken and muscles relax

Absorbing like a dry sponge the first drop of acclaim

Nothing is comparable to this sensation

Spikes of self esteem soon crash craving more

Alone for all the world to see

Alone in his songs of love and glee

Alone in his delight and desire

Alone soaking up his adulations

Ovations esteem melodies and lyrics

Which chart their way through contrived emotions

Some are reflections of his own life

Others histories of heroes past

Alone like the North Star on a misty night

Alone in self and soul, in heart and mind

Alone he wanders to the next hotel room

Alone awaiting the next venue for his adulation fix

John J Roche

An Ounce of Plug

The silhouette produced by well stacked turf fire
   outlined a once well built frame

The well worn suit jacket, with its matching
   waistcoat and the thick corduroys

That once clung tight to taught lean muscle and
   sinew

The decade old cap, only removed to eat or attend
   Mass, veiled a thinning pate

And the sturdy footwear once so light would soon
   feel like a diver's lead lined boots

He sat on the wooden settle by the hearth rubbing
   heat into rhumatised limbs

At a signal only known to himself he dug from his
   pockets the rudiments of his smoke;

The well honed pocket knife, the brown pipe,
   cleaner and lucifers

So began a ritual that had been performed meticulously
for neigh on three score years

In precise detail and well practiced ritual was the rose
wood readied for its aromatic fill.

From the waistcoat pocket he took the black
compressed plug of Virginia's finest

By a well schooled eye he cut a measure to be teased
into fibrous strands;

Ground and massaged, milled and kneaded, between
his work wearied hands

The stem cleaned, the bowl was emptied and stoked
with its new aromatic fuel

And once fired the pipe imitated an altar server's
thurible; incensing the air

Now he would lean back with eyes closed; lost in his
own deliberations

As if induced into an opiated trance reflecting on his
glory days of youth

The friends he cycled with to the momentous games at
Thurles, Kilkenny and Carlow

And after a dance the girls he offered to take home on
the crossbar of his Raleigh

John J Roche

And, ah, sweet Una from the banks of the Nore with
  whom he had made the vow

Reawaking, to our presence from his mental
  gallivanting, he would address the nearest

"Did I tell you about the day when Christy Ring put
  three under and nine over the bar"?

On occasions he would relate anecdotes of great men
  and low, or a tale of my uncle Willow

Or the night when Liam McHugh dared the garda
  sergeant to step on his coat

For long hours we were regaled with many a story all of
  which were reputed to be true.

The man and pipe were indelibly etched into this young
  one's mind and imagination

A mental iconograph that will be treasured as dearly as
  any Byzantine creation

 Unlike the photos in the biscuit tin from the Box
  Brownie that have faded over the years

Lamentably this great book of stories and knowledge,
  one winter's eve, closed for ever

A man's richness is not measured in wealth but the way
  that he walked this earth.

John J Roche

The Seal of Absolution

In Nomine Domine the boy begins

Repeating a well rehearsed formula

Sin is simple for a seven year old

And easy to confess to priest or parent

Scrumping apples, sibling wars, dodging dishes

Pulling pigtails, telling tales, breaking windows

Mea culpa mea culpa mea maxima culpa

The penitent chants

In remorse and sounds contrite

Delinquent adolescent despising moralisations

Struggling for autonomy

Fighting battles indiscriminately

Clamping the youth's will is the gravest sin

Tensions mount whilst peers stare

Mea culpa mea culpa mea maxima culpa

The penitent chants

In remorse and sounds contrite

John J Roche

Clasping hands, the rueful lover

Bends a knee and strike his breast

Fearing separation amplifies contrition

In the emotional hierarchy fear dwarfs guilt

Reconciled with a kiss - the seal of absolution

Mea culpa mea culpa mea maxima culpa

The penitent chants

In remorse and sounds contrite

The husband's ears slowly deafen

The needle scratches the same old groove

Automatic replies lack conviction

Said in a practiced contrite semitone

Like a cathedral chant with no heart

Mea culpa mea culpa mea maxima culpa

The penitent chants

In remorse and sounds contrite

John J Roche

On the deathbed the priest anoints

The sands of his days falling fast

The wounding of hearts in pique or guile

Trouble now a restless mind

Now the veil is rent and the real sin perceived

Mea culpa mea culpa mea maxima culpa

The penitent chants

In remorse and sounds contrite

John J Roche

The Politician

From door to door I do implore

To cast a vote to restore me to the floor

But after taking the oath I do admit

To my promises I can not commit

Mighty speeches where e'er the faithful are gathered

Like a parrot on a high rung perched; party policy
endlessly regurgitated

With a little local issue thrown in to interest and
flavour

The great actor delivers the party manifesto as
salvation for the masses

From door to door I do implore

To cast a vote to restore me to the floor

First take care of my biggest backer

And budget a little money to appease the slackers

Now I'm on the floor the voter is but a boar

For now I'm simply there to be my party's whore

Like the priest prostrate before the ordaining bishop

I bow to the promise of incardination into high office

John J Roche

From door to door I do implore

To cast a vote to restore me to the floor

You must understand that voracity can be grand

But the highest truth is the party policy for which I
stand

I swear to tell as much of the truth as policy will
dictate

And never answer a question which will clear the
slate

But I know in my heart when it comes to the test

I can only take one fork; blind loyalty to the party is
best

From door to door I do implore

To cast a vote to restore me to the floor

Secretly I do admire the independent that fights with zeal and fire

But, alas, ambition for high office blunts a warrior's sword

John J Roche

The Grail Of The Subjugated

There is a drink, a lovely drink

And many deprived of even a sip

They thirst like cracked clay in a desert sun

No man will deny that many will shrink

For the price to grasp this grail

Is poured out in floods of sanguine fire

Many heroic airs intoned in the camp fire rink

By warm home hearths and in ale soaked taverns

Of those who drew courage as from deep stocked caverns

Who took their bravery beyond the brink?

In fighting and winning, or, in loosing and dying

All for a sip of this lovely drink

John J Roche

The Long Winter On Inis Fail

Cold blows

a wind from North and East, that would
cut a man in half

and scatter the sons of Mil from Drom
Caoin

Cold winds

howl and drive relentlessly the tribes
Eriu, Eremon, Ir and Eber

the men who named Inis Fail now
pinned back, go to ground

Cold waves

cross the seas, a squall from France
tossing Angles, Saxon and Jute before it,

ranting and roaring it continued across the
Irish Sea only to settle on the land

Terrible cold

followed in its wake, rounding heads,
driving the tribes of Tara to Lug Plain

from Femen to West Luachar,
many an effort to stem the tide buckled
by such force

John J Roche

A mild stir

brings the West awake to turn the tide of
the bitter cold flow

but from East there is still a vigour,
hanging the protagonists between heaven
and Connaught

 Easter morn

the weather takes a turn with the
Rising of the Son, a new dawn

with the rising,

a warm glow of spring's freedom,
a long winter is abated

John J Roche

The Old Man

Lank and lean, weathered by work in rain, wind and
sun

Now he likes to rest and smoke when his daily tasks
are done

Slowly now he walks e'en tho' his gait is long

But he is not ready yet for a requiem song

Encyclopedic knowledge of local lane and byway

Gallivanted by the likes of Pinch and Caoch O'Leary*

There lives no stranger to him in the parish of
Raheen

Nor ne'er a man cursed by anger from his spleen

*Caoch (quake) O'Leary was a blind piper recorded in the writings of Shanahoe
writer John Keenan 1809-1849

Sixty years of hard farming labour has accumulated a toll

More mellow now instead of the once rigid pole

Aches and pains have grown like wild ivy on a wall

When last at a doctor is too long to recall

The hours by the fire in the evening get longer

The heat brings relief and makes him feel stronger

A game of twenty five is welcomed for his cunning wit

Eyes may have dimmed but the mind is sharp I admit

John J Roche

Despair

I turn in hating and berating

A stain of dark hovers over me

Isolation, isolation, isolation

Peace how I crave thee

Head bent; sorrow bent

Drowning in self's tears

Legs of lead, dragging

Eyes burning, staring

Craving somber sleep

Eternal restless turning

Moping; but slightly hoping

For a new dawn

John J Roche

War Once Again

The dove laments

And dreads the wail

Of innocents weeping

And widows mourning

Combatants clash

Boys blooded to men

Guns flash and bodies gash

Murdering holy innocence

Perennial slaughter

Since the Spartan host

The best of young men

Bled on ambition's altar

John J Roche

Beyond Eden

I sit outside myself

Hardly daring to look in

Remembering words I wish I had not said

Embarrassing now; my cheeks are red

But in the garden of life

There are the roses; my pride

For all who pass by to admire

Qualities that bring social endorsement

A good portion of the garden is in shadow

Hidden from plain sight; best kept that way

There I shilly-shally to bring my lamp

Or linger long on nature's forces

My garden outside of Eden

Needs to be rendered by the hoe

Toil diligently to amend the shadow into light

Hard painful work; don't take fright

John J Roche

The three score years and ten of men

Not enough to make the garden whole

But now I know the shadows like my hand

I can own them as with the roses

John J Roche

*And The Old Triangle**

The Chief ensconsed on his central podium

Surveying troops like a king on the day of battle

Encompassed by captains awaiting orders that drip from his lip

Satisfied, he drops his head to signal the striking of the battle gong

Went jingle jangle all along the banks of the royal canal*

The gong intones and officers bark; unlock, slop out

The muted calm latent with anticipated clamour

Is shattered. Doors banging, thumping boots on plywood landings,

Cadging favours hollered, and noisy cheery banter starts a new day

*Words from Brendan Behan's song The Old Triangle

98

*And the screws were bawling "get up you bowsies and clean out your cells"**

Every day it starts this way and is one less to serve

For today is like yesterday and every other day since

Grey confining victorian walls broker monotonous routine

Days meld, weeks meld; is it June or January?

*I wish to blazes they would raise the wages**

The theorist proclaims "imprison for reform" and thereby initiate rehabilitation

By sewing mail bags to regenerate a new denizen to return to society

It hardly cuts the hay. Politicians whose platform is Law and Order

Merely wish to warehouse and change not a damn bit on any day

John J Roche

The Desiring I

A fire burns deep deep within the soul

Inflaming that naked primal ambition

That wells up in all that the longing spirit espies

Empowering; the lustful must have their coveting

The longing fire fuels uncontrollable craving

Insatiable cavernous lust

Sisyphean daily toil never relieves the gnawing

For each new day dawns a newfangled want

The lustful fire plumes so bright

It blinds the discerning eye

Mistaking tinsel for twenty four carat

As the desiring spirit prances before empty totems

Desire obsessively motivating

Like a legion almost impossible to restrain

Hard work even for one of Plato's philosopher kings

And even those of more stoic persuasions

John J Roche

Noble and yeoman alike stand vulnerable

Besieged, as by a barbarian horde at the gate

But self destruction can be thwarted

Schooling in delayed gratification paves the way

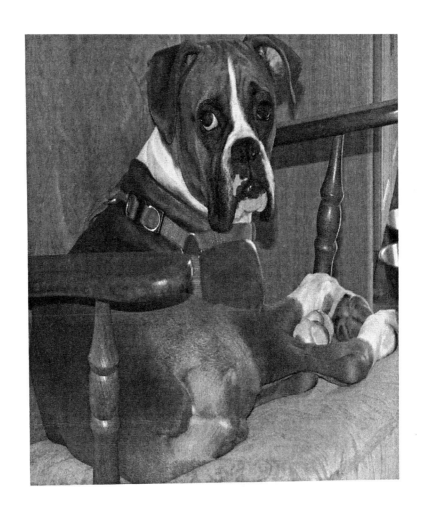

John J Roche

The Pig's Bladder

The pig's bladder sown in leather

Stirs men's passion contesting its possession

Practiced tactics exercised to snatch victory

No quarter given for its total aggression

A just war has been declared

Onlookers squirm and cheer aloud

Offering advice on every move

Square jawed they will not be cowed

Second guessing the other's move

Chess pieces move in anticipation

Armchair experts know best

How to guide a winning formation

John J Roche

Colleen O Ma Croi

I am no William Auden
or Shakespeare t'is true

But I do wish to publish a refrain
which speaks of my delight in you

Spoken on my lips you'll know
it is from a heart true and strong

And without further ado here are
the words of my heart's little song:

You are the light of my eye
which brightens my soul

The beat of my heart
which races when near you

The thought of my mind
and delight of my soul

You are a special friend
walk always by my side

Lyric in Bm

Anne Maria Kelly a girl to love

Blue eyes, black hair, pretty as a dove

On the day we parted you took more than yourself

You left a shell; cracked and broken hearted

Where are you now, where did you go

Here in my heart I love only you

No colour in life, no more spice

The world is cold, cold as blue ice

Like a fire side hearth that warmed me through

I clung to you because I thought your love was true

Where are you now, where did you go

Here in my heart I love only you

John J Roche

Lyric for Wednesday 's Child

Marie Rose, visions impose

Images resonating Michael Angelo

She hides away her beauty and her tears

Deep within the recess of her soul

Marie Rose, I beg, I propose

Don't hide away

Your beauty or your truth

May you wander back some time

Through the memories of your mind

Searching for that truth that lies deep within

That will free the gate of your heart

Marie Rose, visions impose

Images resonating Michael Angelo

She hides away her beauty and her tears

Deep within the recess of her soul

Marie Rose, I beg, I propose

Don't hide away

Your beauty or your truth

Don't be afraid to let somebody love you

Speak tenderly to you

Open your heart

And the loneliness will abate

John J Roche

An Alphabet of People

Amber and black

Flits amiably from bloom to bloom

Hovering, sucking in its needs

Having drunk of the well flies off

Challenge and you'll feel the sting

Bone idle, bone lazy

Slumbers, onlooking, no daring

No subject of history

Dreams of palms and sand

John J Roche

Cow eyes; full round and black

Enticing: enigmatic beauty

Watching

Unrevealing

Seducing, in a blink

Dunces all rushing in

No wit, no reflection

Flotsam and jetsam

No ring needed to lead by the nose

Ever watching all surveying

Eyes darting: radar sweeping

Frightened

Something might be missed

Friendly, forgiving

Soft and round

One Julius Caesar would welcome

Satiated

John J Roche

Ghastly ashen

Contours of pain etched deeply

Crucified

The great suffering was only three hours

Not a life project

Haltingly moves, every step a decision

Cautious

Choice is a curse; paralysing

Decide brother, decide

Insular, inward looking, inferior

Like Paul Simon's Rock

Afraid to chance relation

But alas, no risk no ecstasy

Jock the Scot, flaming top

North of the wall

Fond of the water of life

Only to keep out the cold, mind

John J Roche

Kingly, master of all he surveys

Ambles in studied casualness

Demeanour designer made

Impression is paramount

The real buried under a million fig leaves

Lanky laconic

Hides the frame; no terrier here

No wasted words

Every utterance tardy and deliberate

Moronic

Manly biceps abounding

Makes lots of noise; likes lots of noise

Noise fills the emptiness

Tabloid intelligence

Namby pamby,

Mother's darling

Flower pressing,

Nature's guessing

John J Roche

Overly orderly overall

Meticulous detailing

Pernickety outbursts

All must be just so

Proud and pert: strutting peacock

Displays only for admiration

Audience gobbler

Loneliness pierces deep

Quarrelsome, quirky, insatiably negative

Acid veins strangle generosity

Begets pungent atmosphere;

Under the pretence of being forthright

Roguish rake; likeable villain

Rascally charming the heart

Dangerously disarming evoking sympathy

So watch your jewels

John J Roche

Serious, had a humour bypass

Analysing ad nausea

Rodin's model

Bald of life

Thorny, prickly

Corkscrew mind

Twisting and manipulating

Caveat Emptor

Unctuous, smarmy

Uriah Heep clone

Loathing underpins his pleasing

Betrays with a kiss

Vivacious joy

Vibrant lust for life

High energy and enthusiasm

A joy to accompany

Always surprising

John J Roche

Wandering, wrestles nomad

Never easy with self

Always looks out; never within

No green grass under this one's feet

Xenial and welcoming

Open door and open heart

A generous hearth

Tinctures of accepting grace

Youthful in mind

Never staid

Ravenous for learning

This dog loves new tricks

Zany omadhaun

Small mind great heart

Faithful to a fault

Like the quadruped

A good best friend

Photographs